Fun to Draw

SKATEBOARD *Action*

by Debra Rowley
Illustrated by Ed Francis

D1126982

Published by Hamburger Press
401 E. Wilson Bridge Road, Worthington, Ohio 43085

Copyright © 1989 by Hamburger Press

All rights reserved. No portion of this book may be reproduced,
stored in a retrieval system, or transmitted, in any form or by
any means, electronic, mechanical, photocopying, recording, or
otherwise without prior written permission from the publisher.

Printed in the United States of America

10 9 8 7 6 5 4 3 2 1

ISBN 0-87406-368-X

GETTING STARTED

Learn to draw amazing skateboarding tricks, using the easy, four-step instructions shown here. Study the pictures in the back of the book to learn to draw lots of skateboarders using the correct body positions. On the last page, match the safety equipment to the skateboarder.

DRAWING STEPS

1. Draw the basic shapes lightly with a pencil. Draw guidelines for the nose and eyes. You will erase these lines right before the final step.

2. Draw ovals for the hands, legs, and arms. Make sure the body parts are in the correct positions. The skateboarder must look balanced on the board.

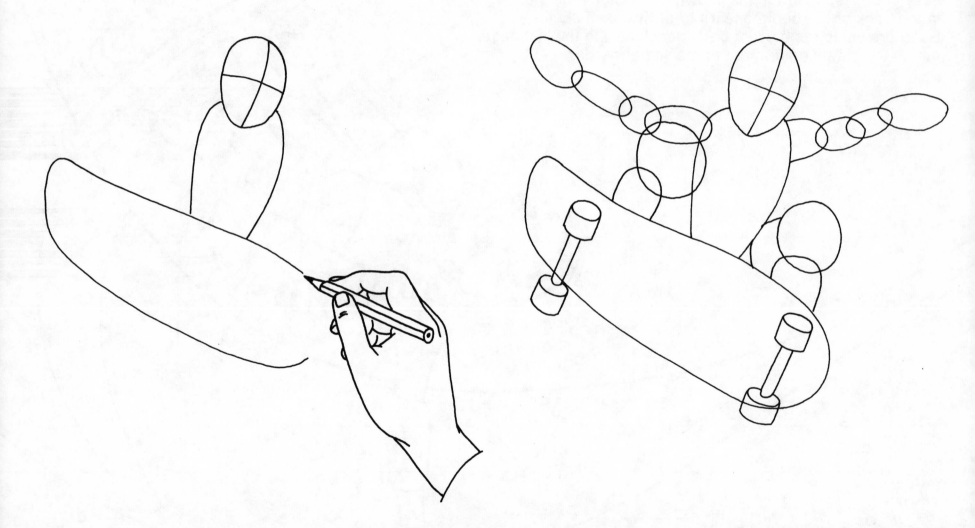

3. Draw bold lines around the basic shapes to finish the different parts. Draw the face. When you feel the drawing is just right, erase the guidelines.

4. Finish the drawing by adding designs and detail to the clothing and to the skateboard. Add motion lines to show speed and movement.

CARVING A LINE

2. Draw shapes for the shorts and the shirt. Draw oval shapes for the arms, legs, hands, feet, and skateboard.

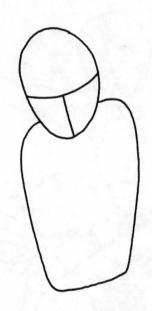

1. Lightly draw an oval for the head, and draw guidelines for the eyes and nose. Draw the body shape.

4. Draw designs on the clothing. Draw a skateboard path and motion lines.

3. Draw the face, using the guidelines. Finish the shapes using bold lines. When you feel comfortable with the drawing, erase the guidelines.

BACKSIDE WALL RIDE

2. Draw ovals for the arms, legs, hands, and feet. Draw a nose line. Then draw an oval for the skateboard.

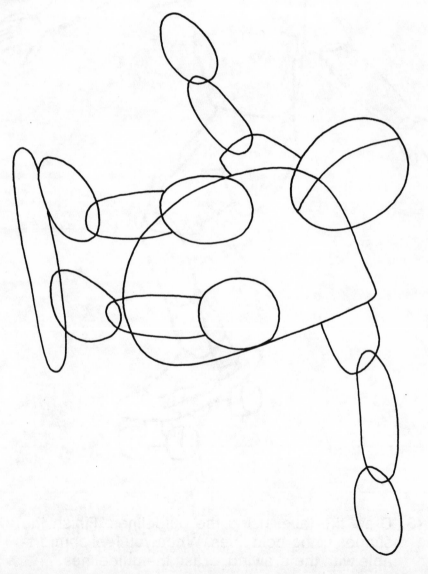

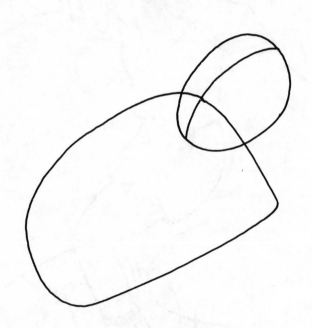

1. This guy is skateboarding vertically! Draw the basic shapes in the proper positions.

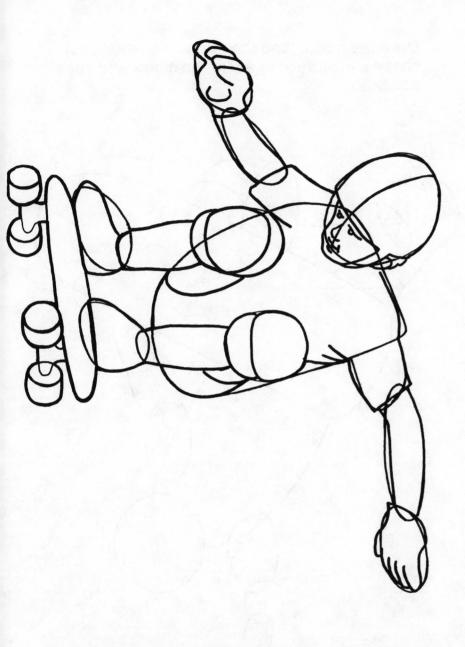

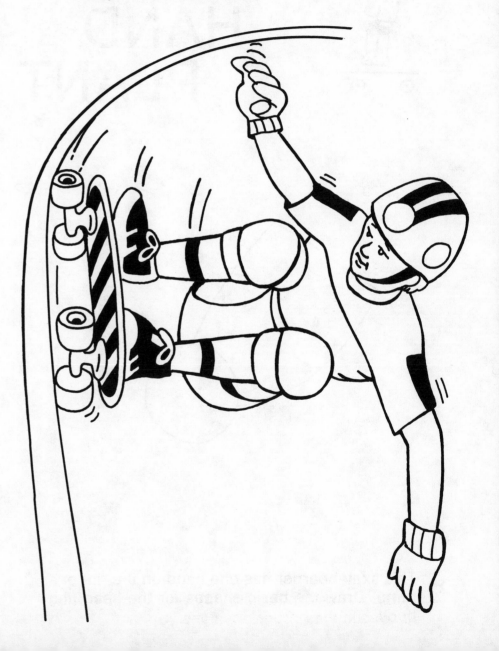

4. Darken in the designs on the clothing. Draw a ramp and motion lines.

3. Using the guidelines, add bold lines to finish the shapes. Draw the face. Be sure to draw the helmet, knee pads, and gloves. When you are finished, erase the guidelines.

REVERSE HAND PLANT

2. Draw the board, and then draw the other body shapes. Include shapes for the elbow and knee pads.

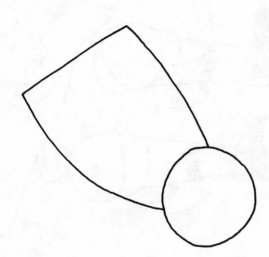

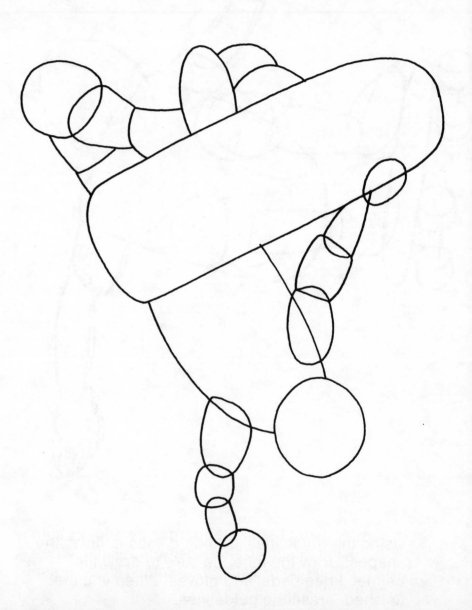

1. This skateboarder has one hand on the rim of a ramp! Draw the basic shapes for the head and body.

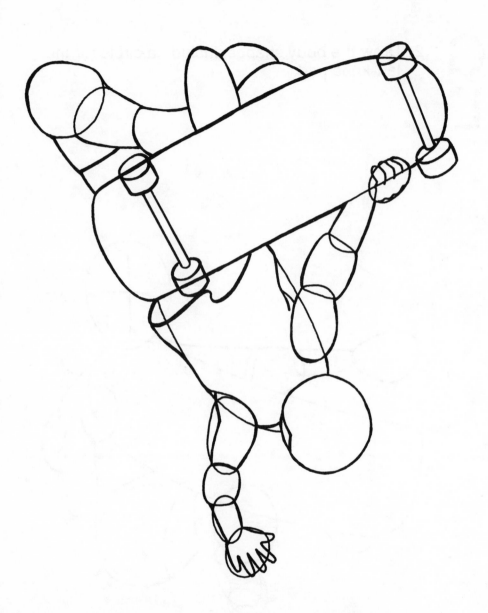

4. Add detail to the clothing and safety equipment. Draw a design on the bottom of the board. Add the ramp's edge, and motion lines.

3. Finish drawing the skateboarder by adding bold lines, using the basic shapes as guidelines. When you are finished drawing the skateboarder, erase the guidelines.

Boosting AERIAL

2. Draw the body shapes. Include a circle for the left-knee pad.

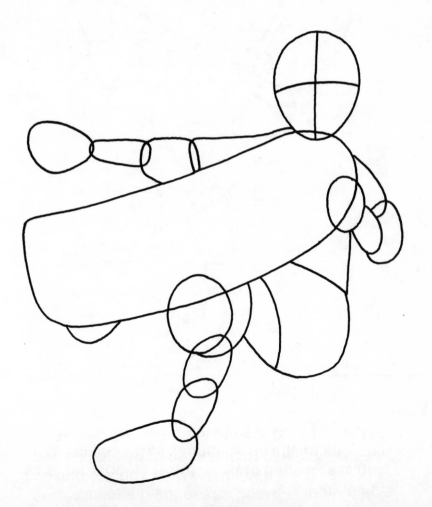

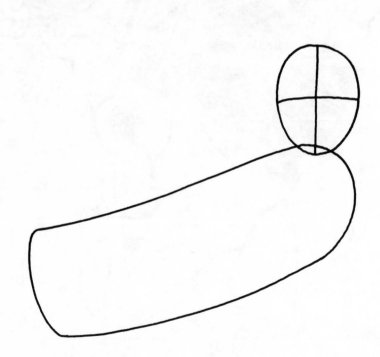

1. Draw this skateboarder holding his skateboard while in the air. Draw the head and board shapes.

4. Draw the ramp. Draw a design on the board, and add motion lines.

3. Use bold lines to finish the body shapes and board. Draw a helmet. When you are pleased with your drawing, erase the guidelines.

KICK TURN

2. Draw ovals for the arms, legs, hands, and feet. Some of the ovals will be guidelines for the elbow and knee pads. Draw an oval for the board.

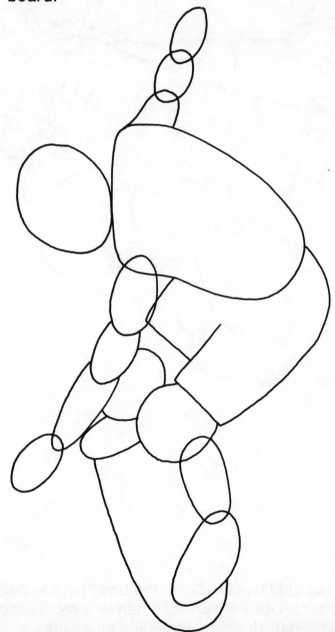

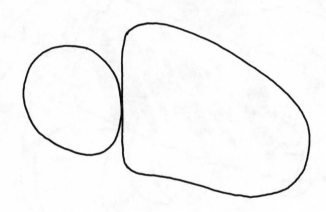

1. Draw the head and body shapes to show that the skateboarder is leaning forward.

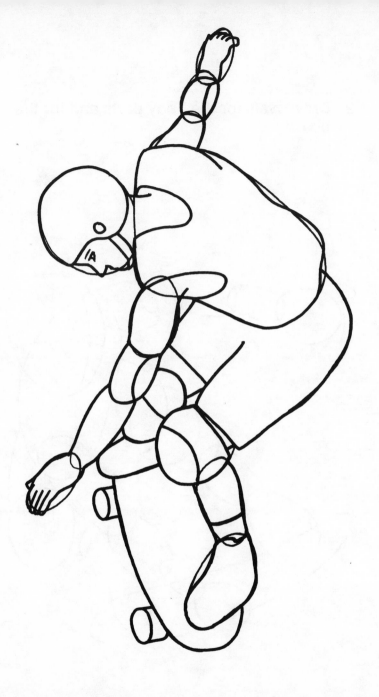

4. Add designs and detail. Draw the skateboard path. Add motion lines.

3. Use bold lines to finish the body shapes. Add safety equipment. When you are ready for the next step, erase the guidelines.

FRONTSIDE AERIAL

2. Draw ovals for the body parts and for the board.

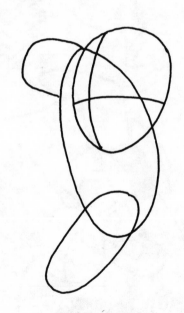

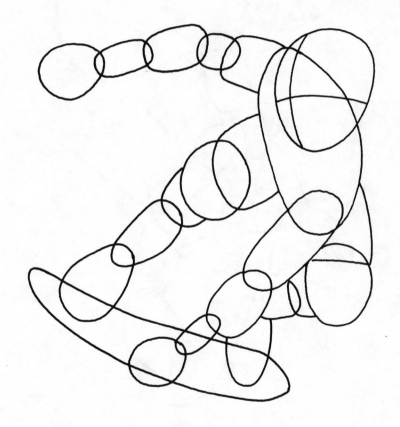

1. This skateboarder is holding onto the front edge of the board. Draw the beginning shapes.

3. Use bold lines to finish the shapes. When you are happy with your drawing, erase the guidelines.

4. Add detail and designs. Draw the ramp and motion lines.

BACKSIDE
TAILSLIDE

2. Draw the other basic body shapes and the board shape.

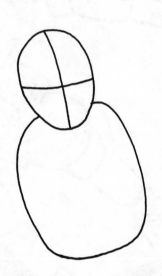

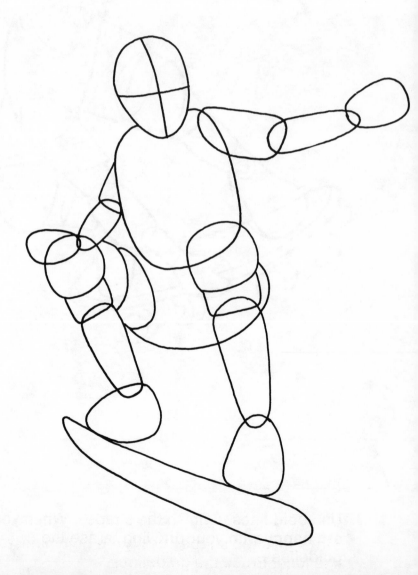

1. *Swoosh*! This skateboarder is going down the ramp. Draw the head and body shapes. Add the eye and nose lines.

4. Draw designs on the clothing. Decorate the board. Draw the ramp and motion lines.

3. Draw finished shapes using the guidelines. Add the face. Erase the guidelines.

FRONTSIDE, NO-HANDS AERIAL

2. Draw ovals for the other body parts. Add wheels to the board.

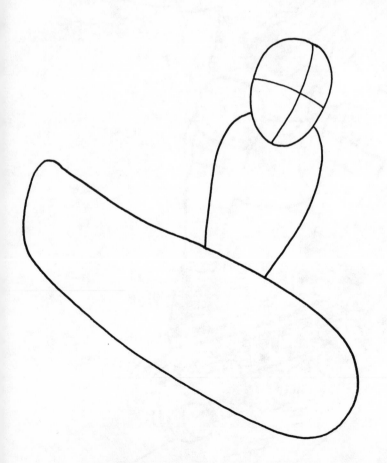

1. Draw the basic shapes for the body, head, and board.

4. Add detail and motion lines.

3. Use bold lines to finish the shapes. When you are happy with the drawing, erase the guidelines.

ROLLING AN EDGER

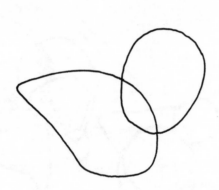

2. Draw the other body shapes and an oval for the board.

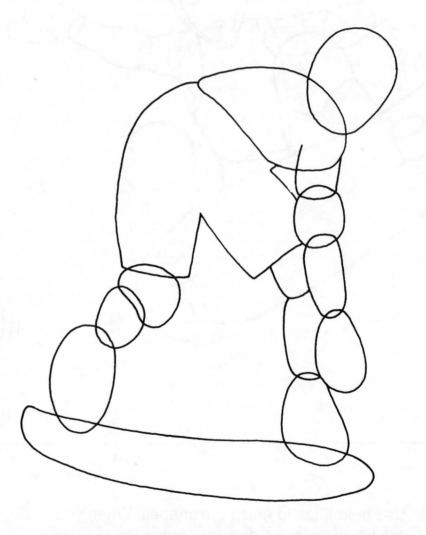

1. Draw the head and upper body shapes.

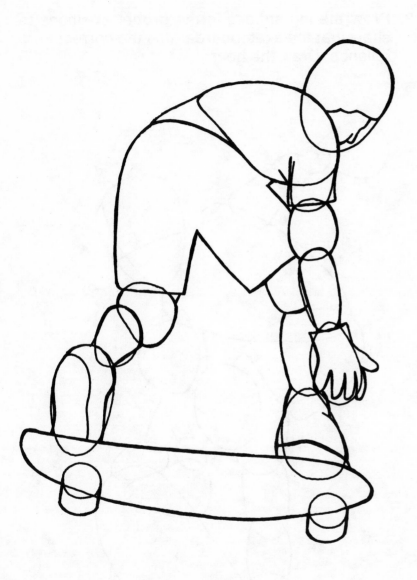

4. Add a wild design to the clothing. Draw the edge of a ramp. Add motion lines.

3. Use bold lines to draw the finished shapes around the basic shapes. Erase the guidelines.

Ollie Off Ramp

2. Draw the leg shapes in the proper positions to show that the skateboarder has the correct balance. Draw the board.

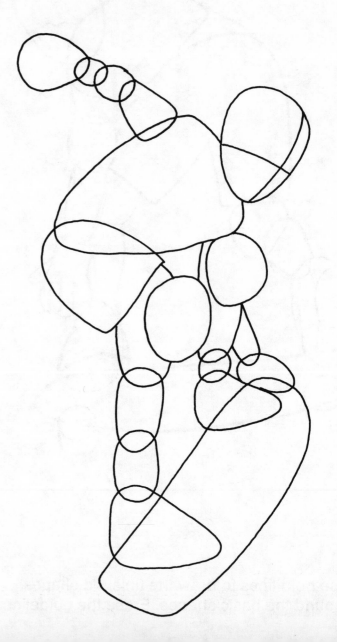

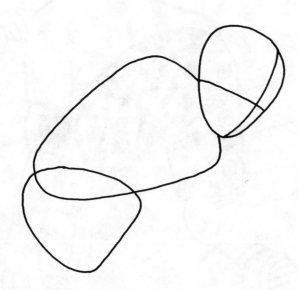

1. Draw the basic body shapes.

4. Add detail. Draw a ramp and motion lines.

3. Draw bold lines for the finished shapes. Use the guidelines to draw the face and hair. Erase the guidelines.

HAND PLANT

2. Draw the other body parts in the proper positions to show that the skateboarder has good balance.

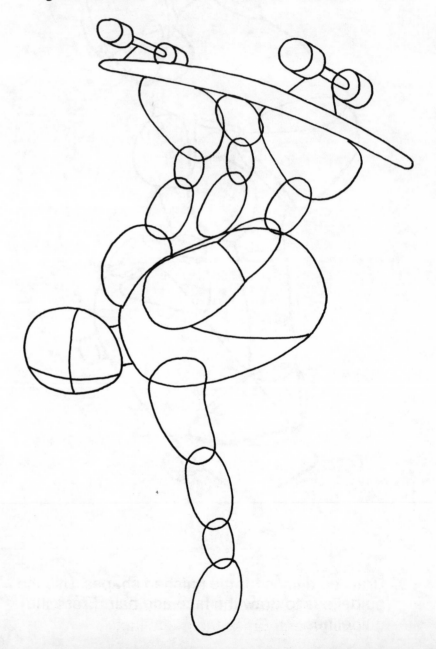

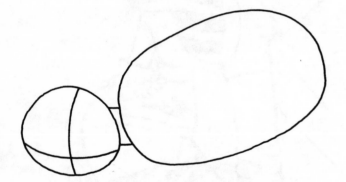

1. Draw the head and body shapes to show that the skateboarder is horizontal in the air.

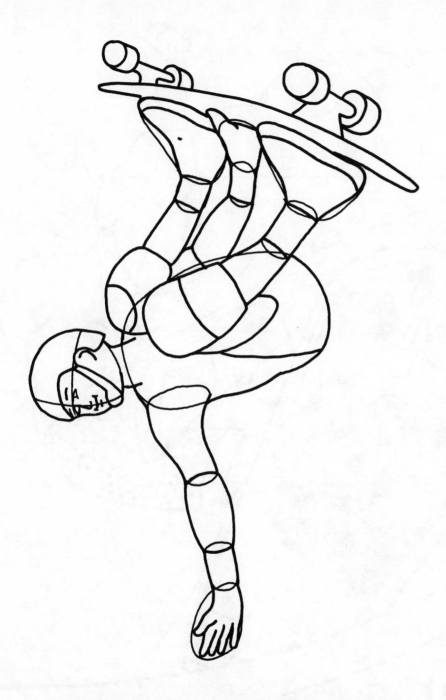

3. Draw the finished shapes, and add safety equipment. Erase the guidelines.

4. Add final details.

OFF THE WALL.

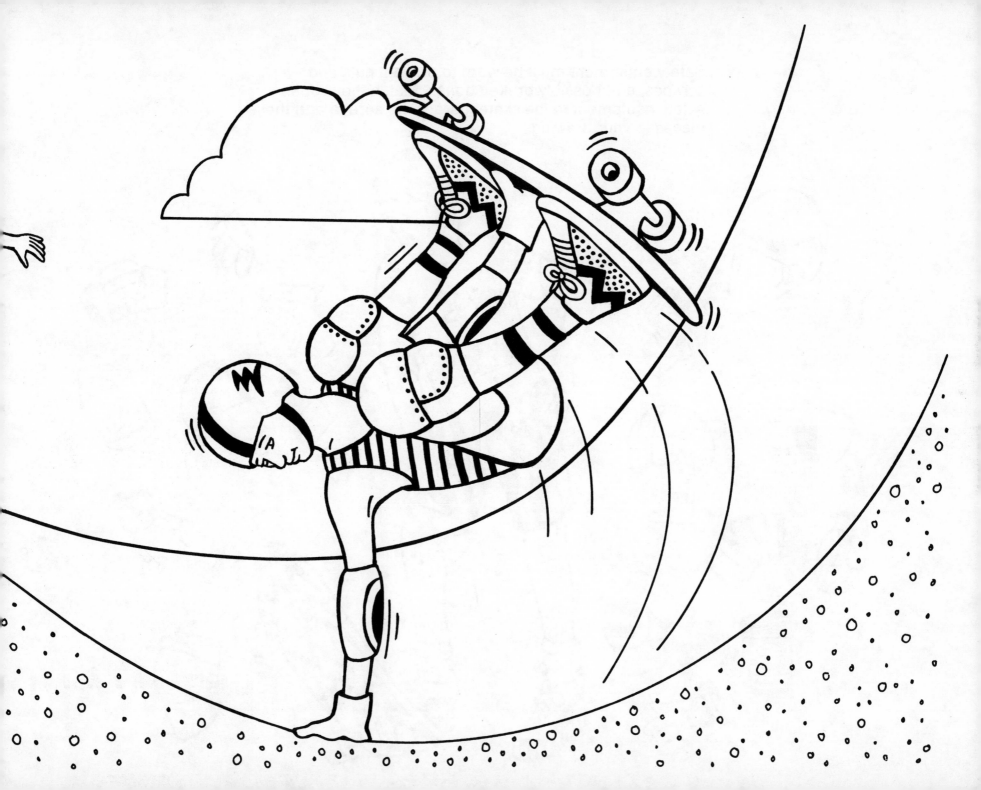

Safety equipment must be worn to prevent cuts and scrapes, and possibly broken bones. Match the proper safety equipment to the skateboarder. Be sure to add these pieces to your drawings.

MAHWAH PUBLIC LIBRARY, NJ

3 9140 09227534 5

DATE DUE

DISCARDED

SUPERMAN LAST STAND OF NEW KRYPTON
volume one

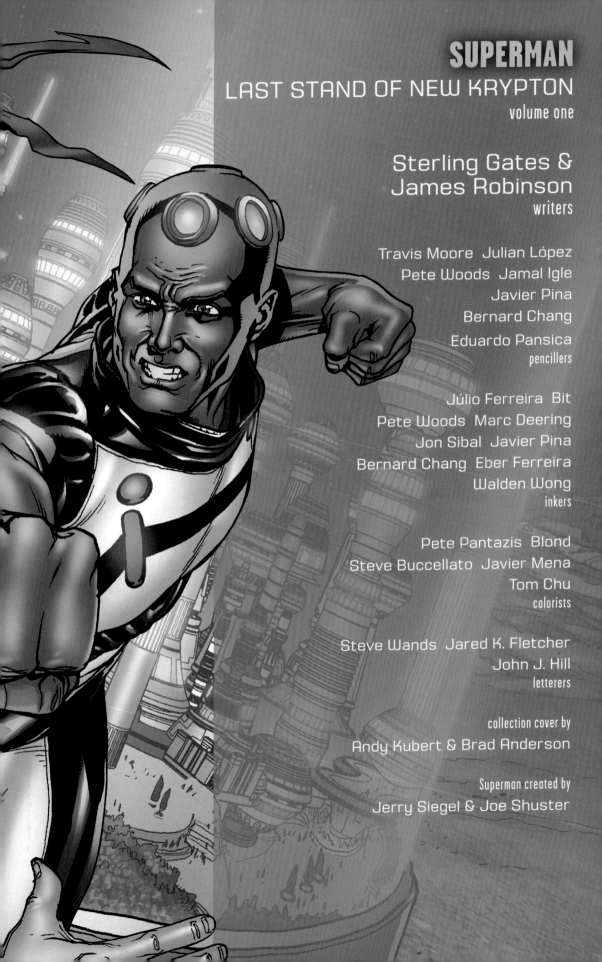

SUPERMAN
LAST STAND OF NEW KRYPTON
volume one

**Sterling Gates &
James Robinson**
writers

Travis Moore Julian López
Pete Woods Jamal Igle
Javier Pina
Bernard Chang
Eduardo Pansica
pencillers

Júlio Ferreira Bit
Pete Woods Marc Deering
Jon Sibal Javier Pina
Bernard Chang Eber Ferreira
Walden Wong
inkers

Pete Pantazis Blond
Steve Buccellato Javier Mena
Tom Chu
colorists

Steve Wands Jared K. Fletcher
John J. Hill
letterers

collection cover by
Andy Kubert & Brad Anderson

Superman created by
Jerry Siegel & Joe Shuster

MATT IDELSON Editor-original series WIL MOSS Assistant Editor-original series BOB HARRAS Group Editor-Collected Editions SEAN MACKIEWICZ Editor ROBBIN BROSTERMAN Design Director-Books

DC COMICS

DIANE NELSON President DAN DIDIO and JIM LEE Co-Publishers GEOFF JOHNS Chief Creative Officer PATRICK CALDON EVP-Finance and Administration

JOHN ROOD EVP-Sales, Marketing and Business Development AMY GENKINS SVP-Business and Legal Affairs STEVE ROTTERDAM SVP-Sales and Marketing JOHN CUNNINGHAM VP-Marketing

TERRI CUNNINGHAM VP-Managing Editor ALISON GILL VP-Manufacturing DAVID HYDE VP-Publicity SUE POHJA VP-Book Trade Sales ALYSSE SOLL VP-Advertising and Custom Publishing

BOB WAYNE VP-Sales MARK CHIARELLO Art Director

SUPERMAN: LAST STAND OF NEW KRYPTON Volume 1

Published by DC Comics. Cover, text and compilation Copyright © 2010 DC Comics. All Rights Reserved.

Originally published in single magazine form in ADVENTURE COMICS 8, 9, SUPERMAN: LAST STAND OF NEW KRYPTON 1, 2, SUPERGIRL 51, SUPERMAN 698. Copyright © 2010 DC Comics. All Rights Reserved. All characters, their distinctive likenesses and related elements featured in this publication are trademarks of DC Comics. The stories, characters and incidents featured in this publication are entirely fictional. DC Comics does not read or accept unsolicited submissions of ideas, stories or artwork.

DC Comics, 1700 Broadway, New York, NY 10019
A Warner Bros. Entertainment Company
Printed by Quad/Graphics, Versailles, KY, USA. 10/20/10. First printing.
HC ISBN: 978-1-4012-2932-0 SC ISBN 978-1-4012-2933-7

SUSTAINABLE
FORESTRY
INITIATIVE

Certified Chain of Custody
Promoting Sustainable
Forest Management
www.sfiprogram.org

Fiber used in this product line meets the
sourcing requirements of the SFI program.
www.sfiprogram.org PWC-SFICOC-260

cover by FRANCIS MANAPUL & BRIAN BUCCELLATO

PROLOGUE PART ONE THE FUTURE IS PROLOGUE
STERLING GATES Writer TRAVIS MOORE Penciller JÚLIO FERREIRA Inker

PROLOGUE PART TWO THE FUTURE IS NOW
JAMES ROBINSON Writer JULIAN LÓPEZ Penciller BIT Inker

I QUICKLY LEARNED.

BRAINIAC 1 WAS MY GREAT, GREAT, GREAT, GREAT, GREAT GRANDFATHER ON MY FATHER'S SIDE.

HE LIVED A THOUSAND YEARS AGO, THE MOST KNOWLEDGEABLE BEING IN THE UNIVERSE.

HE SHOULD'VE BEEN SOMEONE I LOOKED UP TO. INSPIRATION FOR A SMALL BOY WHO NEEDED IT.

BUT BRAINIAC 1 WAS FLAWED. HE DIDN'T EARN THAT KNOWLEDGE THROUGH HARD WORK OR STUDY.

HE STOLE IT.

BRAINIAC CROSSED THE UNIVERSE A HUNDRED TIMES OVER, KIDNAPPING RACES AND BOTTLING THEM UP SO HE COULD FEED OFF THEIR INFORMATION, LIKE SOME PARTS OF OUR CULTURE.

HE WAS NOTHING MORE THAN A THOUGHT-THIEF...

WORLDS DESTROYED
- ARKHEON
- AUROS
- BLIGHT WORLD
- CALUFRAX MAJOR
- CUNDIFF

- DURLA I
- IMSK
- KROP TOP
- LARROD
- LANOTHIA
- LEXOR
- RIMBOR

...AND MY FATHER HAD GIVEN ME HIS CURSED NAME.

"WHY?"

WHY WOULD YOU GIVE ME THAT **NAME!?**

BRAINIAC WAS A **CRIMINAL!** ONE OF THE **THOUGHT-TYRANTS** OF THE 21ST CENTURY! HE WAS RESPONSIBLE FOR THE EXTINCTION OF **HUNDREDS** OF RACES!

HE WAS SO HATED THAT COLU OUTLAWED THE USE OF THE TITLE "BRAINIAC" FOR ALMOST A **THOUSAND** YEARS! UNTIL--

UNTIL I **RECLAIMED** OUR FAMILY'S NAME AND CALLED MYSELF "BRAINIAC 4."

YES, EXACTLY! WHY DID YOU DO THAT, FATHER? WHAT **GOOD** DID YOU THINK WOULD COME OF IT?

BRAINIAC WAS OUR **ANCESTOR,** QUERL. WE ARE HIS DESCENDANTS-- HOWEVER BLESSED OR CURSED THAT MAKES US.

IT'S UP TO **US**--YOU AND I--TO **RETAKE** THAT NAME AND MAKE OUR FAMILY TITLE SOMETHING COLU IS **PROUD** OF.

SOMETHING THE UNIVERSE WILL **ADMIRE,** NOT FEAR.

I **TRIED,** BUT NOW IT'S YOUR TURN. **YOUR** TIME. SOON, THE ENTIRE UNIVERSE WILL KNOW YOU'RE THE **SMARTEST** BEING IN IT.

UNIVERSE? WHAT DO YOU MEAN?

I RECEIVED A HOLOCALL TODAY FROM A MAN NAMED R.J. BRANDE.

TELL ME, BRAINIAC 5. HAVE YOU EVER HEARD OF THE **LEGION OF SUPER-HEROES?**

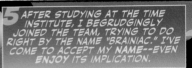

5 AFTER STUDYING AT THE TIME INSTITUTE, I BEGRUDGINGLY JOINED THE TEAM, TRYING TO DO RIGHT BY THE NAME "BRAINIAC." I'VE COME TO ACCEPT MY **NAME**--EVEN ENJOY ITS IMPLICATION.

IT SAYS EXACTLY WHAT I WANT IT TO SAY--

CONNER, ARE YOU UP THERE?

I'M *SURE* HE IS, MR. JANSON. I'M *CERTAIN* I HEARD HIM EARLIER.

DOING HOMEWORK, I BET.

HE SAYS YOU'RE PRETTY GOOD ABOUT IT, BUT MRS. TUCKER IN HISTORY LOVES HER ESSAY ASSIGNMENTS.

CONNER!

YEAH, MA...

...I'M COMING DOWN.

AND SO...

...OF COURSE I TRUST YOU.

THEN COME WITH ME NOW TO *SMALLVILLE*.

SO THEY'RE *ALL* AT YOUR FARM, THIS "LEGION OF SUPER-HEROES ESPIONAGE SQUAD"?

AND *QUITE* A CAST, TOO. NICE THOUGH, ALL OF THEM... I MEAN, STARMAN'S A BIT WEIRD, BUT *APART* FROM THAT...

AND YOU *CAN'T* TELL ME WHAT THIS IS ABOUT?

IT'S *NOT* THAT I CAN'T, BUDDY...

THOUGH *I* CAME HERE *FIRST*.

TO MINE FOR *RICHES*. YEAH...THAT'S IT...I WAS SUPPOSED TO HUNT FOR *OPALS*.

NO. *WAIT*. HUNT FOR RICHES *IN* OPAL.

YEAH. NO. NOT RICHES... *BEAUTY*.

I HAD TO *FIND* BEAUTY... "*THE* BEAUTY." THAT'S WHAT HE TOLD ME.

LET ME TALK, THOM. I'LL EXPLAIN.

BUT *THAT'S* WHAT HE SAID TO ME.

I KNOW, THOM. NOW SHHH, FRIEND, LET ME SPEAK.

YEAH, YOU GUYS SEEMED SO *MUCH* A PART OF MY LIFE THERE.

MY FATHER TOLD ME TO *GUARD* YOU...TO *SQUIRE* YOU.

YEAH, MON, YOU *ESPECIALLY*...HELP YOU TO GROW INTO THE HERO YOU'RE *DESTINED* TO BE.

WELL, THANKS, I GUESS.

AND IF WE'RE *NOT* AROUND ONE DAY TO PROTECT THE UNIVERSE, *COUNTLESS TERRIBLE THINGS* WILL COME TO PASS.

ALL RIGHT, *FIX* THE PRESENT, *SAVE* THE FUTURE. *GOT* THAT, TOO. SO LET'S *BOOK*.

I'M WITH CONNER, *WHEN* DO WE START?

MOST OF US WERE TOLD TO FIT INTO THE WORLD OF METROPOLIS.

AND ME, SMALLVILLE.

YOU, TOO, CONNER, BUT YOU WERE FURTHER ALONG IN DOING THE WHOLE HERO THING. I WAS ENOUGH OF A LOOKOUT--ME AND TELLUS AT LEAST.

OKAY. BUT WHAT'S THE BIG DEAL ABOUT US THAT'S SO IMPORTANT TO THE FUTURE?

WHAT DO YOU MEAN, THE FUTURE'S "IN DANGER"?

AND THAT'S AN ANSWER WE DON'T KNOW. MY FATHER WASN'T 100% ON THE HOW AND WHY. ALL WE KNOW IS THE FUTURE IS FROZEN...IT'S IN DANGER AND YOU'RE A PART OF WHAT FIXES IT.

WELL, TO BE MORE PRECISE, THE FUTURE OF THE LEGION OF SUPER-HEROES.

NOW. THIS THING NEEDS FIXING RIGHT NOW OR WE ARE DONE.

'KAY. WHAT ARE WE WAITING FOR?

YEAH, WHAT PART OF EARTH ARE WE HEADED TO?

EARTH?

JECKIE? WILL YOU?

SURE.

SO, TELL ME, GUYS...

cover by ANDY KUBERT & BRAD ANDERSON

LAST STAND OF NEW KRYPTON PART ONE **INVADED**
JAMES ROBINSON & STERLING GATES Writers PETE WOODS Artist

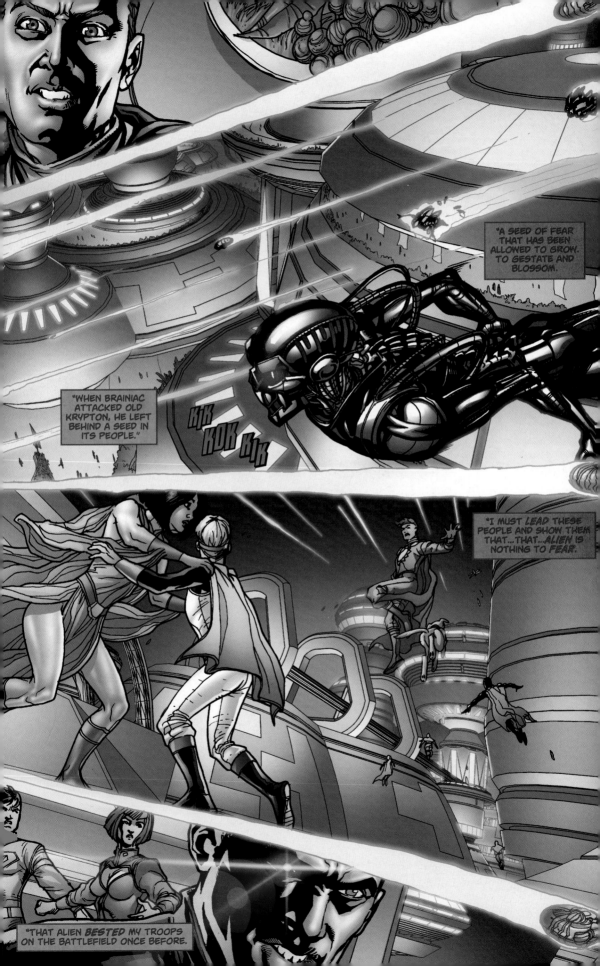

"HE WILL FIND THINGS ARE *VERY* DIFFERENT THIS TIME AROUND.

"HIS FORCE FIELD ISN'T SOLID...IT FLOWS, SENSING ANY LOOMING FORCE AND MOVING TO WHERE IT'S NEEDED.

"THIS LEAVES *OTHER* AREAS WEAKER WHERE THERE IS NO PERCEIVED THREAT.

"...*BEFORE* THE ENERGY SENSES ME COMING AND RECALIBRATES."

"HOW MUCH TIME WILL YOU HAVE?"

"BASED ON HOW FAST THE ENERGY MOVES, I'D SAY, OH...

NOW.

"GENERAL ZOD!"

YOU?!?
NO--

"THE RETURN OF
BRAINIAC." "KRYPTON VERSUS
BRAINIAC." "BRAINIAC'S REVENGE."
DID YOU *REALLY* THINK *THAT'S*
ALL THIS *IS?*

cover by JOSHUA MIDDLETON

LAST STAND OF NEW KRYPTON PART TWO **LEADERS**
STERLING GATES Writer JAMAL IGLE Penciller MARC DEERING & JON SIBAL Inkers

NEW KRYPTON HAS BEEN INVADED.

BRAINIAC HAS **RETURNED** FOR US.

HE WANTS TO **UNDO** ALL OF THE THINGS WE'VE **BUILT** OVER THE LAST YEAR.

ALL WE'VE **ACCOMPLISHED**.

HE WANTS TO TAKE US **BACK**.

I SAY--

THOOM

MOTHER, ARE YOU *ALL RIGHT*--

≥KAFF≤ *≥KAFF≤* I'M *FINE*, KARA.

D-DID YOU *KNOW* THAT BOY?

THAT'S *CONNER.* KON-EL. HE'S KIND OF PART OF OUR *FAMILY.* WHY WERE YOU--?

HE'S PART OF AN *ALIEN* TERRORIST GROUP THAT'S BEEN *RUNNING RAMPANT* THROUGH OUR CITY.

I SAW THE *HUMAN* D.N.A. IN HIM AND OUR HOUSE CREST ON HIS CHEST AND I ASSUMED HE WAS *ANOTHER* ASSASSIN, AS SUPERWOMAN WAS.

COUNCILOR *ALURA.*

WE'VE JUST RECEIVED WORD THAT OUR GUARDS HAVE *SUCCEEDED* IN *RECAPTURING* THE OTHER ALIEN *TERRORISTS.*

THEY'RE *NOT* TERRORISTS, THEY'RE THE *LEGION OF SUPER-HEROES.* THEY'RE HERE TO HELP *FREE* THE "BOTTLE CITIES OF BRAINIAC"--

KIK KAK KIK

GENERAL ZOD HAS BRANDED THEM *TERRORISTS* AND ORDERED THEM *ARRESTED* ON SIGHT, KARA ZOR-EL.

NOW STEP OUT OF MY *WAY.*

AS YOU *RECALL,* BRAINIAC SEEMS TO HAVE *TARGETED* YOUR MOTHER, AND WE HAVE ORDERS TO ESCORT HER TO SAFETY--

cover by JULIAN LÓPEZ, BIT & SANTIAGO ARCAS

LAST STAND OF NEW KRYPTON PART THREE DESTINY
JAMES ROBINSON Writer JAVIER PINA & BERNARD CHANG Artists

"...BUT APART FROM THAT, WE KNOW NOTHING."

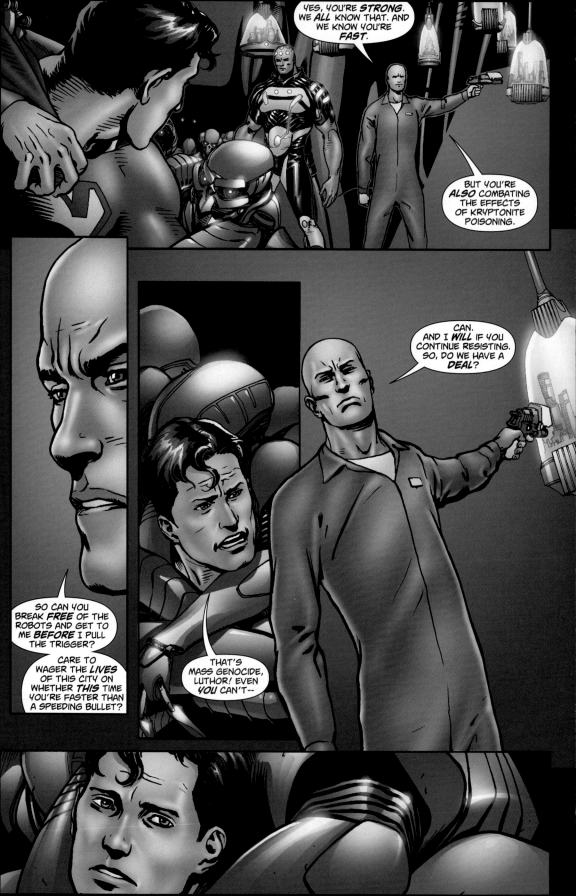

cover by JOE QUINONES

LAST STAND OF NEW KRYPTON PART FOUR
NAMESAKE
JAMES ROBINSON Writer TRAVIS MOORE Penciller JÚLIO FERREIRA Inker
UNIFY
STERLING GATES Writer EDUARDO PANSICA Penciller EBER FERREIRA Inker

...BY AVERTING SOMETHING THAT, BASED ON *EVERY HISTORICAL RECORD,* IS *NOT MEANT* TO HAPPEN IF OUR PRESENT NOW, *TODAY,* HAS ANY HOPE OF *CONTINUING.*

THAT EVENT IS THE *DEATH* OF *SUPERMAN.*

BRAINY, *SPEAK,* BUDDY! *COME ON!* HOW YOU DOING?

YES, CHAMELEON BOY'S ESPIONAGE SQUAD IS ALREADY *BACK* IN THE 21ST CENTURY...

...BUT THERE'S *NO WAY* THEY COULD *KNOW* THAT EVENTS IN TIME HAVE *FURTHER CHANGED.* THEY NEED TO BE *WARNED.*

I THINK OF HIM. *ME.* THE *NAME* I CARRY...

BRAINY! *SAY SOMETHING!*

TELL US *WHAT* TO DO!

...AND ALL OF THOSE WHO'VE COME BETWEEN.

BRAINIAC.

HIS REAL NAME LOST TO TIME.

HIS MOTIVES...WAY BEYOND THOSE OF ANY OTHER COLUAN. YES, WE ALL SEEK KNOWLEDGE ABOVE EVERYTHING ELSE.

BUT WITH BRAINIAC, IT WAS MORE.

A GREED TO TAKE WHAT HE LEARNED AND KEEP IT. HIS ALONE.

SHRINKING CITIES...ONE FROM EACH WORLD HE'D FIND. ONE CITY. BOTTLE IT. TAKE IT. KEEP IT.

AND THEN DESTROYING THAT WORLD AND ALL OTHER LIFE AROUND IT.

EVIL. BRAINIAC. PURE EVIL.

HIS CLONE WAS LITTLE BETTER.

VRIL DOX.

YES, HE FORMED L.E.G.I.O.N. AND LATER R.E.B.E.L.S.-- BOTH FORCES FOR GOOD...

...BUT SCRATCH THAT PATINA EVEN A LITTLE AND IT'S CLEAR, FIRST AND FOREMOST, THEY WERE MAINLY GOOD FOR VRIL DOX.

EVIL OF MANY TYPES WAS FOUGHT AND FINISHED BY THE ACTIONS OF VRIL'S TEAMS.

BUT HOW MANY DIED OR WERE HURT OR HAD THEIR LIVES AND HOPES AND WORLDS SHATTERED FOREVER...

...AT THE GUILE OF BRAINIAC 2?

HIS SON. LYRL DOX. BRAINIAC 3.

SMART AND CRUEL, AT FIRST.

LATER, SMART AND SAVAGE.

A LITTLE BETTER.

YES, WITH EACH KEEPER OF THE MANTLE BRAINIAC, A LITTLE BETTER.

WHEN VRIL DOX EVENTUALLY DIED, A VICTIM OF HIS OWN HUBRIS AND TREACHERY...

...FEW MOURNED, MOST REJOICED.

BUT AS FOR BRAINIAC, THE FIRST, THE WORST...

...HIS ULTIMATE FATE--LIKE HIS "GRANDSON'S" --IS A MYSTERY.

HE MAY HAVE DIED...OR TRAVELED THROUGH TIME TO THE 31ST CENTURY TO PLAGUE US NOW AS PULSAR STARGRAVE.

OR...SOME CLAIM HE WENT BACK TO THE BIRTH OF CREATION ONLY TO HAVE HIS MISERABLE LIFE SNUFFED OUT BY AN ANCIENT POWER GREATER THAN HIS.

YES, HE MAY HAVE DONE A LOT OF THINGS.

BUT THE ONLY THING WE KNOW... ABSOLUTELY KNOW...

...HE DIDN'T KILL SUPERMAN.

AND UNLESS HE'S STOPPED, TIME AND SPACE WILL END.

THERE'S ONLY TIME TO CALIBRATE FOR THE BODY CHEMISTRY OF ONE PERSON TO BREACH THE TIME LOCK.

AND MY ANCESTOR MAKES THIS MY MISSION.

MARS IS GONE, BRAINY. COME ON!

IS THAT WHY I'M THINKING ABOUT THE PAST AND OTHER PEOPLE'S LIFETIMES? THE WEIGHT OF EXISTENCE ON MY SHOULDERS.

NEW KRYPTON.
THE 21ST CENTURY.

KIK
KIK
KOK

OH,
GREAT--

cover by GEORGE PÉREZ & HI-FI

LAST STAND OF NEW KRYPTON PART FIVE BOTTLES AND BATTLES
STERLING GATES & JAMES ROBINSON Writers   PETE WOODS with TRAVIS MOORE Pencillers   PETE WOODS with WALDEN WONG Inkers

"...THEY HAD BETTER HOPE THAT *BRAINIAC* KILLS THEM BEFORE *I DO*."

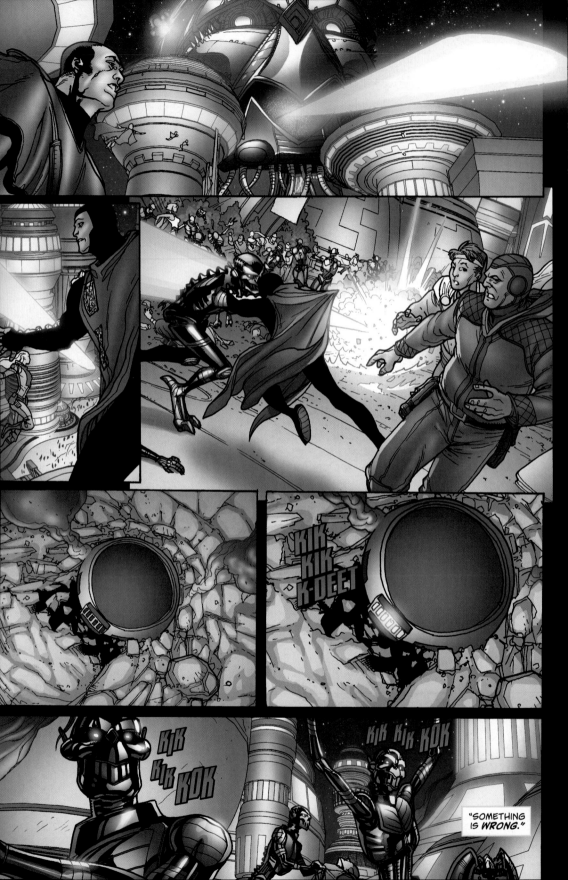

KIK
KIK
K-DEET

KIK
KIK KOK

KIK KIK KOK

"SOMETHING IS *WRONG*."

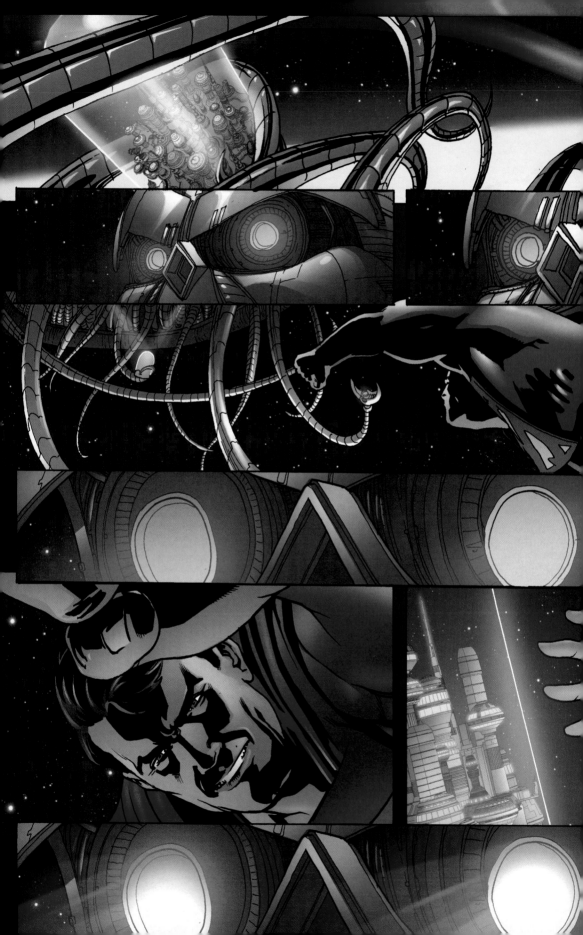

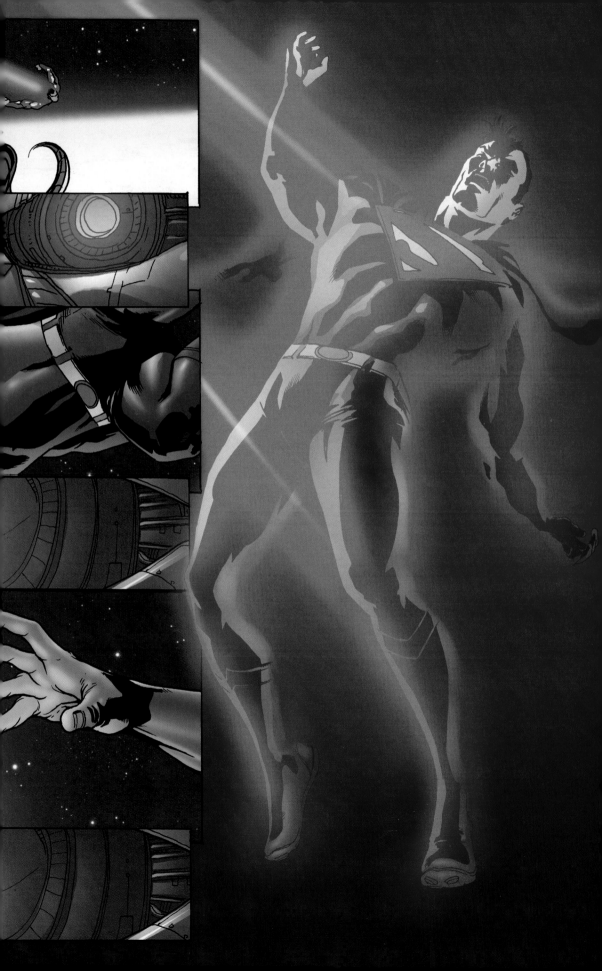

Andy Kubert's original cover to SUPERMAN: LAST STAND OF NEW KRYPTON 1 features Superman in his New Krypton military uniform.

Red Sun Probot

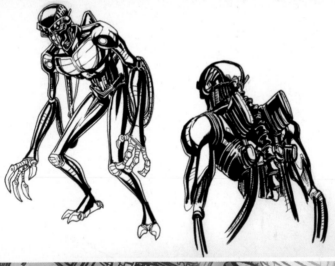